fool proof romance

Love Between the Beat Sheets

christopher downing

mad devil media

For all the clients who fired me, who reminded me it's better to teach than be a know-it-all.

what to expect

We're going to touch on four significant aspects of romance stories:

romantic tension,

romantic structure,

characters,

and happy ever afters.

Those are the significant tools of the trade.

However, we're not going to do a deep dive on all of them.

In fact, we'll spend most of our time on the most important aspect of romance: romantic tension all by itself. And that's because…

Everything from structure to characters to happy ever afters serve the tension.

And if everything else serves the tension, then tension comes first. Don't forget that. It's the boss. All things bow low before it.

Lots of romance writers start with structure. Why? Because there's some truly eye-opening books about it, and because beat sheets are really, really handy.

But you can follow structure for 20+ novels and still not fully grasp how to pack your stories with nail-biting, nerve-blowing, heart-pounding tension. And somewhere in the middle of your 21st book, you'll sense that. You might still be wondering, what the hell am I even doing? Some of you have even retained a writing coach, and I have met you, and you've allowed me to practice the material in this book on you, and I am grateful :)

On the other hand, if you first understand how tension works in romance stories, structure will become second nature. Then you'll liberate yourself from pre-ordained templates. Or not, if you don't want to. But at least you'll be free to choose. Once you understand how romantic tension works, what its sources are, how to draw it out, how to inflame it, then you're going to get a lot more out of using beat sheets.

Structure will become merely a tool you use to make all the romantic tension even more explosive and satisfying.

Lastly, this book doesn't contain a whole lot of Shoulds. You *should* do this. You *should* do that. As I've learned over the last decade, there are few things more detrimental to one's creative spark than all the world's Shoulds. Anyone who says you *should* do anything has their own agenda. Maybe it's a good agenda. But it's theirs, not yours.

I'm not trying to create a writing system for you to take on as your own. Please don't expect that. I've done that in the past, and I've learned that everyone's brain works differently and everyone has a different process. There is no foolproof system. However, these are foolproof concepts. Learn these concepts and you can apply them to your own system, your own process.

What I provide here are options.

Find what works for you.

Then do that.

A lot.

ice breaker

So LET's dabble with some romantic tension. In this chapter, you'll brainstorm and write out a summary of a very simple romance. Even if you don't think you know anything. This is a simple, hands on demonstration to feel what it's all about.

As you read through this book, you'll see more of these ideas, and things will get more complex. However, for now let's keep it simple. And build as we go.

Below are some bare bones steps I want you to follow for this demonstration. If you do, you'll get a very simple, halfway decent summary of a romance.

I encourage you to write out your responses to the steps in narrative form as I do in the example, as opposed to bullet points or lists. After all, we're writing here, as in prose, not merely plotting. So write a few sentences per step.

Ready?

For now, here are your types of romantic tension and the bare-bones steps to follow.

- Family/Social Pressure
- Actively at Odds

1. Describe two main characters (MCs).
2. Pick a trait or two they like about each other.
3. Pick one of the above sources of romantic tension.
4. Pick another attractive trait they eventually learn about each other.
5. Use the other source of romantic tension. Make it worse.
6. Decide how they overcome those obstacles and stay together.
7. Finally, describe why life is better in love.

Take a stab at the steps on your own. Maybe even before you read my example below. Just try! It's alright if things feel clunky. It's your first time. If you make a few attempts, I bet you'll get a better feel for it each time.

Here's an example. I'll make it up as I follow the steps.

1. Describe two main characters (MCs).

Meet Samson and Marge. Samson was a high-dollar, high-stakes attorney who's enjoyed all the bad things the press said about him. Marge was a low-level, lowly-connected journalist trying to get her big break in a cut-throat industry.

2. Pick a trait or two they liked about each other.

Marge was immediately interested in Samson, who naturally seized command of his team, and everyone around him worked as hard as he did. Samson noticed that Marge was a clever problem-solver, requiring her to be a keen observer and quick on her feet. Also, both looked really good in jeans. Duh.

3. Pick one of the above sources of romantic tension.

Problem was, Samson had a reputation to uphold. His team,

his colleagues, even his dad who still was a firm partner, questioned his command as he cavorted with enemy #1, the press. Marge on the other hand, had a dominating editor who had serious rules about fraternizing with sources. All eyes were on them, growing suspicious by the day, the more they 'interviewed.'

4. Pick another attractive trait they eventually learned about each other.

Marge knew how to ask powerful questions, and before long, she understood Samson's rebellious side, that he'd always been held to an impossible standard, that his recklessness was his way to escape the world of high-stakes, often corrupt power games. At the same time, Samson eventually learned that Marge's altruistic core regularly hobbled her journalism career, that she often covered vulnerable communities instead of writing popular, click-ready news stories.

5. Use the other source of romantic tension. Make it worse.

Things came to a head when Marge's suspicious editor discovered she'd been involved with Samson, and Samson's suspicious father discovered he'd been getting vulnerable with the media, and dark family secrets were now in jeopardy. The editor demanded Marge go public with what she knew—as well as her source, Samson. The dad demanded Samson prove his loyalty, using Marge to spread propaganda about a rival, or else he was out of the family business and on the street. Both Samson and Marge had good reasons to fear these consequences and suffered for their mixed loyalties.

6. Decide how they overcame those obstacles and stayed together.

Ultimately Samson rebelled completely, leaving the corrupt world of the family law firm behind rather than betray Marge. Marge had gone so far as to write the exposé her editor demanded, tears all over her keyboard, but couldn't hit the publish button. Samson kicked in the editor's door and told her to back off; same time, Marge called the editor and on speakerphone told her that she couldn't betray her source because she loved him and screw her and screw this business. Samson was in the editor's office hearing it all. Samson told her to meet him on the roof, where they embraced, his helicopter coming down behind them in dramatic fashion. It picked them up, and off they went. Together.

7. Describe why life was better in love.

Six months later, they were in the small, humble office they shared. Samson was now focused on underprivileged clients, taking civil cases that others wouldn't touch, slowly becoming the bane of slumlords. Marge was the muckraker, finding dirt on those who abused their power and privilege, often helping Samson with his cases, and she was gaining her own reputation. They didn't make a ton of money. But they were making a difference. In the end, they're holding hands, declaring they wouldn't have it any other way when there's a knock on the glass door, and through the door they see a mother holding a baby with two toddlers at her side. They reach for the door together—and open it.

Not too bad, is it? It's got good bones for a novella. A longer novel has room for more complications, more side-characters, and more back Sand forth. Admittedly, I got a little carried away with deets at the end, but that's what happens when a story goes from nothing to heartfelt.

Did you feel the push and pull developing? The intensity rising? That's what we'll cover.

The point is, this little summary has the elements of a solid romance: romantic tension, characters with powerfully likable traits, a heartwarming HEA, and a structure that got us there.

It's equally notable that there's a *ton I left out*. Any idea what the external plot was? Me neither. Was it insta-love or slow burn? Dunno. How about the heat level? You're free to use your imagination. None of that mattered. Why? Because there were legit qualities that drew them together and two legit predicaments that pulled them apart. And they were structured to create an up-down, up-down dramatic effect. With those alone, it was a romance.

That's about as foolproof as you're gonna get.

Now back up to those bare-bone steps.

Read through them again. I dare you to come up with five different romance stories with five different couples. No, I double dog dare you.

For now, use the same two types of romantic tension I listed; they're common and easy. Dress them up based on different characters you imagine. Try another genre too, why not?

Don't get caught up with external plot. Nor too much back-story. Your goal is to come up with legit romance stories with as little as possible. Primarily with romantic tension. Because that's really all you need for now.

Remember, you're not plotting your next book here. You're learning. Experimenting. Playing. Getting silly.

Move on when you've done it five times. I'll be waiting for you patiently on the next page.

Have fun!

A special note just for you.

I know you didn't complete the exercise five times. I'm watching you.

However, if your job is writing romances, then know that those who write and write and write and practice using new ideas will be better at writing romances than those who skip experimentation. I've seen this go both ways countless times.

Don't merely collect how-to's and checklists. Use them. Play with them. Intuit them. And not just on things you plan to publish. This is how you learn—and prepare yourself to succeed in a highly competitive market.

Also, don't make me lecture you. I don't mind. But you will.

part one

It's All Romantic Tension

what is romantic tension?

I WON'T ASSUME you know everything.

Some of you might be a little hazy about regular ol' tension, let alone the romantic variety.

OK, let's start there. It's pretty important. Tension.

Tension is the expectation of something. Preferably something with a lot of emotions wrapped up in it. Like a girl waiting for a birthday present. Or a woman looking desperately for her best friend at baggage claim. Or a man crawling frantically out of a half-sunk elevator, knowing the cable will snap at any second, and if he doesn't get all the way out in time…

The highest emotions come from the anticipation.

That's tension.

Romantic tension is waiting for things you hope happen in a romantic relationship. Like the long stare before a first kiss.

Not only are we exhilarated by the possibility, there's also a chance it won't happen. Like he'll get scared and look away. That she won't kiss him even if he summoned the courage to try. Or that the door will open, and the chance will be gone, for*ever*.

Creating reasons MCs like each other is fun. Who doesn't enjoy writing chemistry-filled banter? However, creating increasingly troublesome reasons your MCs stay *apart* is a nail-biting good time for the reader.

Simply put, great romantic tension is knowing the lovers absolutely must end up together but *not* knowing how in the world they're gonna pull it off.

A good romance writer will have the reader rooting for the lovers but pulling their hair out because they can't see a path to the happily ever after.

You want readers pulling their hair out.

And you do that with romantic tension.

Let's keep going.

types of romantic tension

THERE ARE 9 types of romantic tension. As a writer of romance stories, there's nothing more important than understanding the 9 types and being able to use them liberally. Every significant trope can be broken down into versions and combinations of these. We'll actually do that together in the next chapter.

You're more than likely aware of these in your own way. You probably have a sense of them, and you'll sure know them when you see them in someone else's book. But that doesn't mean you can remember them when writing your own. Maybe a handy dandy, concise list will help?

Hopefully, after this you'll have a clear enough idea to use them yourself. Intentionally.

A short romance can get away with using only two types of romantic tension. A novella? Say, five. But a full-length novel has room for all nine.

If you're writing a 80K word, full-length romance novel and you're employing only one or two, say a wounded heart with trust issues, you can definitely do better. And when I say better, I mean give your readers more reasons to do that hair-pulling, nail-biting thing.

It doesn't matter if you write sweet Amish romances or

scorching hot contemporary erotica. These are the concepts that will make your stories more emotional, more intense, and more unforgettable.

For quick reference, here are the 9 Types of Romantic Tension.

- **Family/Social Pressure**
- **Social/Cultural Differences**
- **Actively at Odds**
- **One's Misdeed**
- **Internal Resistance**
- **Misunderstanding**
- **Misplaced Feelings**
- **Contrary Feelings**
- **External Wedge**

Let's break each down. It won't take long. See how many you recognize from your own stories or your favorite books.

Family/Social Pressure

Your MCs are madly in love with each other, but there's one big problem: everyone else is totally against it. External pressure can come from all sorts of powerful places: close-minded parents, class hierarchies, religious groups, judgy friends and mentors. If MC1 falls for someone outside of her community, there will likely be people who'll urge her to cool it. They might not only urge her, but threaten her. They might even threaten her new lover. This type of romantic tension has huge potential to make your MCs feel as though the whole world is against them.

Social/Cultural Differences

More of an internal resistance, this is also based on MCs who find love outside their comfortable communities. Everyone else thinks she should date the wealthy entrepreneur, but privately she loathes the idea of rich, entitled men who are used to getting what they want, and she just can't see herself with one. Another form can be an extreme fish out of water scenario, like a British nanny hired by a sheik, where some of the cultural and religious differences would feel truly insurmountable.

Actively at Odds

Your MCs are after the same job. Or they're both race car drivers. Or one is running away and the other is paid to track her down. You want explosive tension? This one's for you. They might not start off as enemies, but just wait. In order for any sort of relationship to work, every other important thing in their lives is on the line. Or at least on hold. And that ain't gonna fly for either of them.

One's Misdeed

Somebody's been bad. And what better time to dredge that up than during a new relationship? Sure, that handsome motorcycle club leader has a hidden heart of gold now, but wait until his new, small town girlfriend discovers what low-life deeds he did to get there. Yikes. And we're not just talking about motorcycle gangs and mafia romance either. Lots of people have made sketchy choices in their past. Or even during the relationship. Loving someone means loving all of their past. That can be tough.

Internal Resistance

The wound. The flaw. The lie they've been telling themselves for years in order to get through life. This type of romantic tension has been dominating romance for awhile—for good reason. Something inside of your MC is broken. Not only can't she live her best life, but she can't love anyone truly either. Yes, she better fix that. Or get the help of a wild, shape-shifting alpha who sees past all her curvy insecurities. You want angst in your romance? Give everyone wounds. For wounds are not healed overnight. And love, compassion, and a sexy reason to move forward are all good medicine.

Misunderstanding

This is an easy one to use, but it can make you look lazy if you use it flippantly. Say your MC1 overhears only half of a conversation, the bad half. Or he misinterprets MC2's gesture. These things can be solved if only they talked about it. But what if MC2 is intentionally ambiguous? What if MC1 needs to keep a secret and is forced to lie? Misunderstandings can be heart-wrenching, as long as the resolution isn't as simple as talking about it like adults.

Misplaced Feelings

MC1's heart is already taken. There's no room for love. Not with MC2, anyways. Maybe MC1 is in a relationship with the wrong person. Maybe he's dedicated to his special ops team. Maybe he's a workaholic, determined above all to solve this latest string of murders. Or maybe he's a pastor, and his heart is pledged to his faith. The reader needs to know that MC1's heart's desire is a viable contender, not simply a jerky ex who keeps showing up. Will he finally choose MC2 over everyone and everything else?

Contrary Feelings

The problem with falling in love with a bad boy is that they're bad. And the more MC1 learns to love MC2, the more she discovers what bad really means. The more she loves him, the more she despises him. The more she craves him, the more she fears his cruel side. Yeah, a dark lord of the underworld looks good in armor and has pledged to protect her, but dark lords do lots of brutal things. She needs to process a plethora of opposing feelings if her fated mate is gonna work out.

External Wedge

This sort of thing involves a dramatic physical separation. She gets reassigned to a different city. His visa runs out. Her space cruiser crashes on her way to him. He gets kidnapped by the rival mafia family, and they've got his feet in a bucket of drying cement. It's like distance making the heart grow fonder—but on crack. Jack up the stakes, and you'll make this type of romantic tension a great go-to for the second half of any romance.

Some of you might find these eye-opening. Some of you might already have insights to all of these types. But I hope this break-down clarifies things.

Feel free to reread this chapter a bunch. For these are the foundational ideas we'll build everything else upon.

The real question is, how do you use them to create amazing romance stories?

Awesome. Glad you asked. Let's keep going.

major tropes and romantic tension

Do you have a few favorite tropes?

Real quick, for those who aren't sure about them, tropes are recurring concepts. Anything can be a trope if it pops up over and over in different stories. From characters types to settings to plots to reader fantasies that go all the way back to *Jane Eyre* and *Pamela*.

If you have a favorite genre, it's probably because you adore the tropes that show up regularly. One might even say, tropes define the genre.

Same with romance.

So. What genre do you plan to write in? What are the genre's tropes that you want to play with? These are good starting questions.

I'm going to list a small handful of romance tropes, or types of stories. I've seen other lists that contain over a hundred. However, these here are just a few of the more recognizable ones. They're types of stories that are super duper popular, and most genres can tweak them to fit as their own. Anyways, they're good for what we're doing here.

- *Enemies to Lovers*
- *Friends to Lovers*
- *Fated Mates*
- *Second Chance*
- *Secret Romance*
- *Fake Romance*
- *Sexy Rich*

Now we're going to feel out these tropes one at a time, and see which of the 9 types of romantic tensions jump out at us. This is a fantastic way to start building a story, long before you worry about external plot stuff.

Know the genre, a general idea of your characters, and the major tingly tropes you want to include—then get serious by figuring out all the ways to create romantic tension.

Think about which of the 9 types of romantic tension apply to the tropes you're going for. Then blow them the hell up. This is a really effective way to begin brainstorming a romance.

Often, the best tropes—hence the most popular—have tension built right into them. That's helpful. Despite that, many recent romances focus on the internal resistance, the wound. In truth, even without a wound, there's plenty of ways to confound love—and more explosive ways too.

Let's go down that short list of popular tropes and identify which of the 9 types of romantic tension exacerbate our MCs, and try things out.

An *Enemies to Lovers* romance might include:

Actively at Odds: they're enemies for a reason, and only one of them can be the winner, and the closer they get to the finish line, the more enemies they become.

One's Misdeed: enemies are perceived to do bad things, sometimes to each other, and if you're looking for reasons to get your feelings hurt, it's never hard to find them in an enemy.

Social Pressure: each MC will have people in their corner, naturally talking smack about the other, and despite their best intentions, they are *not* helping the situation.

Social/Cultural Differences: enemies have qualities—whether perceived or real—that are hard to get over, and if you don't like somebody, like really really don't like them, everything they do bugs you to the point furious madness.

Contrary Feelings: the more they compete, the more intense all those enemy-ish feelings get, frustrations grow into resentments, which grow into despising, which grow into good old fashion loathing.

A *Friends to Lovers* romance might include:

Internal resistance: who wants to ruin a beloved friendship? Better to cling to the status quo and not risk it.

Misplaced feelings: somebody is very likely committed to the wrong person or institution; but remember, no cheating.

Contrary Feelings: frustrations can arise if one MC falls in love first, jealousies can erupt, or enabling friend-zone behaviors can make true love feel impossible.

A *Fated Mates* romance might include:

Contrary Feelings: MC1 is usually all in, while MC2 needs a lot of convincing, and usually MC1 has some nefarious paranormal/alien/alpha/bad boy qualities that make actual true love harder to achieve than that first irresistible hook up.

Social/Cultural Differences: in all likelihood, one MC is a human swept away into the crazy, not-mundane world of the other MC, who is very likely—and very problematically—not human.

One's Misdeed: and boy oh boy do these non-human MCs have backstories, often violent and difficult to get past.

Internal Resistance: no matter how hot MC1 is, MC2 is on some level wholly, and understandably, resistant to being told whom to mate with.

A *Second Chance* romance might include:

One's Misdeed: something happened to spoil the *first* chance, maybe somebody made a choice, maybe somebody left for college or got deployed or absolutely couldn't pass up her chance on the rodeo circuit—and somebody's heart was broken.

Misunderstanding: maybe the reasons why it didn't work out were never clear, and very likely those issues are still yet to be addressed now that everyone's lives are messier and more complicated, sooo that'll be tricky.

Family/Social Pressure: somebody or somebodies were around to see that first heartbreak, and no one wants to see it again.

Internal Resistance: maybe that first breakup led to a pattern of breakups, and now the heart is wary of love and all its complications; or maybe MC1 has lied to himself all these years as to why it didn't work out, and that deeply rooted lie must be unwound.

External Wedge: whatever's brought them together for a second shot at love is right there waiting to pull them apart, like a career or a deployment. Visiting one's home town is just that—visiting.

A *Secret Romance* might include:

Family/Social Pressure: forbidden love is forbidden by *somebody*, and the more powerful, the higher the stakes.

Internal Resistance: living a lie is hard, and lots of sacrifices must be made, and at some point, at least one of the MCs has to ask, is this really worth it?

Social/Cultural Differences: what if those forbidding the relationship kinda sorta actually have a point? What if the MCs themselves start to question their compatibility?

A *Fake Romance* might include:

Misunderstanding: if there was ever a trope synonymous with a comedy of errors, it's a fake romance—because every lie will require a whole slew of lies to keep up pretenses, and that keeps your MCs desperately scrambling in Kerfuffleland.

External Wedge: this charade can't go on forever, and a ticking clock looms, and at some point, something has to give.

Social/Cultural Differences: why are they faking it in the first place? Shouldn't they already be together in love? Your reader thinks so; why don't your MCs?

Contrary Feelings: but then things get serious when the more they fake it and the more they must share that fancy hotel room, the more they realize what's wrong with each other, and cute pet peeves become disastrous.

A *Sexy Rich* story might include:

Social/Cultural Differences: your MC has seen both Pretty Woman and 50 Shades, like, a million times, but really? Lifestyles of the rich and not-rich are so culturally different that your MC might as well be dating an alien—and we're talking either MC, by the way.

Internal Resistance: maybe MC1 is clinging to the status quo because it's safer, or maybe MC1 thinks that MC2's class status makes MC2 untrustworthy, and MC1 must discover what's real and what's a false perception.

One's Misdeed: say MC1 finally realizes that not all rich people are bad and now she's willing to give MC2 a real chance...except guess what? he *does* have a past—and not a pretty one either—and the actual past is worse than she'd ever imagined. Way worse.

. . .

For a foolproof way to brainstorm your romance story, explore the 9 types of romantic tension one by one. Imagine all the different ways you can frustrate your MCs. Depending on what sort of story, some of the 9 types will leap out at you or they might be inherent in the trope, like the examples above. But explore the not-so-obvious too. Dig up ways to confound them!

Again, a full length novel has plenty of room for all 9 types of romantic tension. Some will be major, and some can be minor. Some will be apparent during the first few chapters, and some can show up as the story gets serious.

At this point, you may even begin to imagine bits of scenes. Intense dialogues. Or what huge reactions your MCs might experience when those conflicts show up.

Great. This means you're developing your story, and your story is being built upon romantic tension. If you're an outliner, you might begin taking notes. If you don't like outlining, keep sitting with these ideas, for they will continue to flare.

Except wait. We've got all these reasons our characters might struggle in their relationship, but what makes us so sure they actually want to be together in the first place?

Wow. That's a really good question. I'm impressed with your insights.

We better keep going.

what about the woo?

For a lot of you, characters come first. Before everything else, you like to know who they are, where they come from, and what their goals are—and of course, their wounds. Some of you like to have cover images made up to give you a visual. Some of you take your characters to the coffee shop for little chitchats. Some of you even like using well-thought out character sheets for brainstorming. I love all that. Just like beat sheets, these are great story development habits and tools. Keep doing these things.

Remember, I'm not here to change your process or offer a new system. Instead, I'm here to offer concepts that will empower your process even more.

If you like to start with your characters, cool. Let's do that.

We've already covered attributes that create conflict, like those cultural differences or wounded hearts or naughty pasts. But what about the good stuff? The stuff so powerfully attractive that hearts ache? And therefore all those resistances are exacerbated?

There are always sparkly eyes and cute booties. However, I bet you can handle those booties without me. So let's get deeper.

. . .

As I like to do, here's another simplified clear list, this time of Power Traits. Don't take this list lightly; it consists of the most important positive attributes in town.

In other words, when one human is drawn to another human, it's always because he or she possesses some combination of these qualities.

Yes, MC1's hot abs start MC2's engines, but these are the attributes that make MC2 want to finish the race.

Here ya go.

Power Traits

- Quick to seize command
- Confident, and therefore unpredictable
- Curious
- Idealistic, passionate, and therefore courageous
- Betrayed, rebellious, and therefore independent
- Altruistic
- Resourceful, clever, and quick thinking
- Experienced and skilled

As a guide, I suggest picking 2 or 3 per person. And really emphasize them. Some of these qualities will be more dominant in a person, and they'll show up early on. And maybe one will need to be discovered by the other person as a story progresses.

When you're brainstorming characters of a romance, this list is a fantastic starting place because it gives the other character something to notice. And the reader too.

So when you're figuring out each MC, pick some of these power traits, and daydream how they'll manifest in their lives, their jobs, and their other relationships. They'll need to *do things* that showcase these attributes. In front of each other. Start imagining what those *things* will be, what events bring them out. You might just be imaging scenes that end up in your story.

As you noticed, this time I didn't give a bunch of examples of each positive quality. For one, I think you know what these are. And for another, I want *you* to brainstorm your own examples. Using your own imagination. It's time. Character creation is a deeply personal part of our craft, so start working these things into your own process now. Not later.

(For a quick example, go back and see how I did this in the Ice Breaker. Try to identify which qualities I used.)

Can you see how this is leading towards woo?

Give your MCs strong, legitimate reasons to be attracted to each other, reasons so magnetic that the pull will still exist even when they're struggling and furious in the second half of the story. Go below the surface. Go beyond the squee and grab them by the woo.

The attributes I've listed in this section will seriously help with that.

Just remember, keep some positive qualities hidden. At least for awhile. That will give your MCs things to discover about each other. And who doesn't love surprises?

Later, when we get to structure, we'll chat about how to tease out such things throughout your story. For now, learn these power traits well and use them to brainstorm your characters— and more importantly, their specific actions and choices these traits bring out.

If anything, you're increasing the chances that your readers will take notice. You want your readers falling in love just as much as your MCs. Because what your reader feels is as important as what your characters feel.

Let's do a quick review.

You've picked your genre and your lovers.

With the 9 types of romantic tension, you've brainstormed good reasons they should stay away from each other.

With the power traits, you've dreamed up big reasons they long for each other beyond initial attraction. With those two energies, you've created a dramatic dynamic, a push and pull that keeps everyone guessing, keeps everyone shifting directions, and keeps everyone turning pages.

Well, that's nice. We know your lovers will eventually sort things out. That's a given. That's the promise. But what if…

What if you take each little flickering fire of romantic tension —*and pour on a buttload of gasoline?*

ways to increase romantic tension

IN THE HEARTS and minds of the reader, you've created a romantic mystery. How are these two swoondogs possibly going to end up together? Yeah, they're totally into each other—or at least everyone knows they should be—but look at all these cards stacked against them. Hopefully, you've made the mystery difficult to figure out. Because you've put romantic tension in there. Therefore, the happy ever after that's been promised—not to mention the fulfillment of those reader fantasies—seems unattainable.

Is the reader pulling out their hair yet? Eh. Maybe.

You want to make sure they are. You want *rising intensity*.

Rising intensity is how you keep the up-down, back and forth romantic mystery from getting stale. Especially for a longer story. In the case of your romantic mystery, think of rising intensity as that crazy guy who shows up in the middle of the swanky dinner, stands on the table, and waves around a sloshy can of gasoline. We need resolution—or all hell's gonna break loose!

Come on, I'll show you what I'm talking about. Below are the 15 Intensifiers of Romantic Tension.

- *Use Conflicting, unsettling, or provocative imagery*
- *Take something important away*
- *Offer a temptation not to seal the deal*
- *Slip in misdirection or denial*
- *Explore the what if*
- *Make the status quo less tolerable*
- *Emphasize a character with a conflicting goal*
- *Use indirect or confrontational dialogue*
- *Force it/Adhesion*
- *Make an emotional threat*
- *Up the stakes*
- *Pile it on*
- *Sacrifice another character to demonstrate danger*
- *Make a physical threat*
- *Throw in the ticking clock*

By the way, I ordered this list with rising intensity. Did you sense it? That means that the lower half of the list are the real shaker-uppers.

Remember back in the Ice Breaker when I said your options will get complicated? This is that time. Just remember, your readers like complications.

There are 9 types of romantic tension. The above list gives 15 ways to increase *each* type. Each type!

Don't do the math. But if I were to walk you through every combination, this chapter would get ridiculous. So if you don't do that math, I won't spell out every option at your disposal.

How about just a few tips, so you get the idea, OK?

OK.

Just the tips.

Let's take a story that uses **Actively at Odds** as one of its sources of romantic tension. In this type, two MCs are competing for the same thing. Even though they're attracted to each other, there can only be one winner. That's gonna put a damper on their long-term love prospects. Now, to make the romance more and more exciting, let's add complications—rising intensity—to that single type of romantic tension as the story progress.

Here's my on-the-fly brainstorm of all 15 intensifiers.

Type of Romantic Tension: **Actively at Odds**

Here's the premise. MC1 knows there's a valuable relic in a cave on a high mountain top. MC2 also knows about the relic and must retrieve it for the temple before MC1 can steal it. If one succeeds, the other fails. Love will definitely screw that up. The race is on!

Use Conflicting, unsettling, or provocative imagery

Hostile mountains. Bitter cold. Avalanche threats around every turn. Metaphor potential is as abundant as millionaires climbing Everest.

Take something important away

MC1 is using a GPS to get through the mountains, increasing her odds of winning over MC2. But guess what? She loses it. Better yet, MC2 steals it from her. Dick move!

Offer a temptation not to seal the deal

MC1 gets a call on her radio. Her buyer will pay her more if she quits and retrieves some jade dagger from Chichen Itza. If she leaves the story, she could make more money. Ha, not likely. She needs to pay good-looking MC2 a visit and get her GPS back.

Slip in misdirection and/or denial

After a lusty, uncomfortable dream about MC1, MC2

convinces himself of the race's futility. His own desires will mess up the natural order of things. Why not let those who thrive on greed suffer and get their karma? Better that than keep facing his growing lust for MC1!

Explore the what if

Same time, MC1 has this fantasy where she and MC2 actually get together. It's really sexy for a moment, but then…she loses her contract, her reputation, and for what? Some goody-two-shoes who couldn't possibly keep her fast-paced heart happy? Nice fantasy, but no way.

Make the status quo less tolerable

Except this is a lonely life. For both of them. MC1's buyer has a long list of jobs that will keep her globetrotting and ultimately even more lonely. And MC2's abbot promises a wonderful life of asceticism and celibacy and complete isolation if only he beats MC1. On some secret level, both MCs want to quit and walk away from this life. Which also means they'd never see each other again.

Emphasize a character with a conflicting goal

Now's a great time in the story to dive into each competing MC's motivations. The source behind their need to win. Who is more determined? Does MC2 need the relic to save his brother's life? Does MC1 have a massive debt to repay? Surprise! This race against each other just took on a whole new level of oomph.

Use indirect or confrontational dialogue

Once again, they cross paths on the mountain. Yes, the hilarious chemistry-filled banter is there, but now there's an edge.

They've had fantasies about each other, and they need to prove to themselves that this fight is seriously on. Wicked insults and insinuations are unleashed. They might actually fist-fight. Luckily, the storm rolls in, and they must separate. Whew!

Force it/Adhesion

Except wait. One of the two shelters has been destroyed. By whom? Doesn't matter. There's a wild storm kicking up snow drifts and dropping temperatures. MC2 isn't about to let MC1 actually freeze to death. Grudgingly, through the gale he invites her in. She considers freezing to death a better option, but ultimately she goes in his shelter. And it's a tight fit. And MC1's clothes got wet and need drying. And of course, there's only one sleeping bag.

(PS The race to the relic itself is also an early adhesion, keeping them both in the story, but this one is more fun to talk about.)

Make an emotional threat

Whatever happened in the sleeping bag, they share some endearing, open-hearted pillow talk. During that vulnerable conversation, they find they have a few major things in common, like a love of artifacts and mountain climbing, but the convo also reveals how much they have to lose if the other acquires the relic. Their entire lives are wrapped up in this adventure. Self-worth. Purpose. Identity. Big stuff.

Up the stakes

Next day after the storm, someone knocks on the door, and guess what? Another agent of MC1's buyer has been trailing her. He tells her that the distrusting buyer has decided to put the pressure on her. If she doesn't steal this relic and repay her debts, he's gonna send some goons to visit her ailing father. She doesn't want her failure to get her dad hurt, does she? And don't forget MC2's sick brother who needs the relic's healing properties. They find out he's getting worse.

Pile it on

The last day of climbing is the hardest. Of course. They face all sorts of alpine disasters. Like one thing after another. Over and over, both are continually faced with the harsh, brutal, freezing reality that the mountain will kill them. They are both taken to their physical limits. Do they help each other? Sabotage each other? A little of both?

Sacrifice another character to demonstrate danger

In a dramatic act of selfishness, the buyer's agent tries to get ahead, endangering everyone's lives and, of course, he dies a wonderfully fitting death near the top. But in doing so, he's made the last leg to the summit impassable.

Make a physical threat

Both MCs come together, hold hands, and look over the icy chasm they must now cross. The rope can only support one of them. And it needs to stay intact for the return. They've come so close to the relic, and the mountain has reaffirmed everything: only one of them may pass. They cannot do this together. The chasm *between* them is as perilous as the precipitous chasm before them. Slowly, they pull their hands apart.

Throw in a ticking clock

The winds increase. The dark clouds swirl all about the summit. Once again, snow begins to fall, as does the temperature. The break in the storm is over. If they stay on the mountain much longer, they will both die. What do they really love? What are they willing to sacrifice? Is either strong enough to do what needs to be done to finish this? Faced with this ultimate dilemma, shivering from the cold and swaying with vertigo, they must make their choice. Now.

There. That's fifteen ways to increase a single type of romantic tension.

Remember, in this example I only worked with **Actively at Odds**. Not too shabby for a short story or a novella. However, a full-length novel can use much more than that. What if we introduced other forms of romantic tension from the 9 types? Say, social pressure from the abbot and fellow priests? Or MC1's past misdeeds, like artifact dealing which is loathsome to MC2? Or heck, why not give both of them wounds from their mysterious pasts, internal resistances that make love as impossible as the mountain? Each one of those can also be amplified with the 15 intensifiers of romantic tension above. Whew! That's an awesome amount of potential for a romance.

Maybe too much. Put like that, things start to feel unmanageable. We don't want that.

In reality, if we were to write a full-length romance, we'd—

—use as many types of romantic tension as we could

—but apply only three or four of the intensifiers to each type.

Not all fifteen like I did in the above example. And not an any specific order. That was for illustrative purposes. And for some OTT fun.

When we get to structure soon, we'll go over how to pace out all of these types of romantic tension and all those ways to intensify them—one scene at a time.

For now, I want you to begin understanding how powerful

romantic tension can be, how much story potential you can harness by brainstorming just that.

In the mountain climbing example, you'll notice that some external plot elements emerged. There was an artifact dealer and an ailing dad and a precarious career choice, and there was the sick brother and whatever forces were at play at the temple. It's important to note that those elements arose only because I was exploring the romantic tension. I didn't come up with any of that beforehand. *The external plot was the product of brainstorming the romance.* In other words, romance first, external plot second. I wasn't trying to shoehorn a romance into another plot. Not only does it read more like a romance that way, it's actually a lot easier.

In this chapter, we covered the 15 intensifiers of romantic tension. I created a slightly unrealistic narrative for illustrative purposes, to give an example of each of the fifteen.

Are you eager to keep going? You might have a sense that you're stranded on a mountain and you need to know the ending. Great. You need resolution. You need a happy ever after. Don't we all.

Follow me.

happy ever afters for the win

THE HAPPY EVER AFTER IS WHERE you leave your readers with the best feelings possible. Simply put, you want your readers to know that your lovers have made the right choices and sacrifices for love. You want to *show* the lives of your lovers are better together.

Like zero doubts.

These are the last pages of your story, and you want readers emotionally satisfied—and wanting another experience just like that (and clicking on that link in the back matter).

What role does the HEA play in this? It's not the climax. It's not the big sacrifice nor the big show of commitment. It's not anyone fighting for anything.

On the contrary, the HEA shows things at peace. When the lovers are sure the fight was worth it. When they deeply feel that life is now better because they are together. The fight is over. The fear is gone. The wounds are healed. Your job as a romance writer is to show them in that state—convincingly.

Convincingly? You mean, like in a foolproof way?

Yes, yes I do.

For this, we're once again dipping into the world of human psychology. Bare with me.

When someone is on a journey of positive growth, even a romantic one, they are usually working to fulfill one or all of 5 needs, which I will share in a sec. So when someone is feeling truly happy with themselves, their lives, and their environment, all 5 needs are met.

In a romance, a satisfying HEA shows that the choices and sacrifices they've made on their romantic journey have landed them in a place fulfilling all 5 needs. Either by themselves, or even better with the care and support of their lover.

These are them.

- *Most basic: food, shelter, rest*
- *Safety & security: safety from harm, means to get resources, a safe place to call home*
- *Love & Relationships: friendships, intimacy, family, connections*
- *Esteem: self-respect, respect from others, community status*
- *Empowerment: being the best version of one's self, living one's best life*

And you thought all an HEA needed was a town potluck with some babies thrown in.

Actually, that's pretty darn close. You must watch a lot of Hallmark movies. As cheeseball as they can be, Hallmark knows how to HEA like nobody's business. Even if you write wicked paranormal romance with a dark side, you can still take a lesson from the science behind their time-tested success.

Powerful happy ever afters touch on the alleviation of fears, the fulfillment of needs, and the attainment of joys—more than just love.

Again, the list of 5 needs is an especially good tool to brainstorm what ending will leave your characters truly happy. Even better, this type of ending has far more potential to stir the feel-good emotions of your reader too, to fulfill their fantasies.

Oh, you say you want a few examples? Of course you can have a few examples. Let's jump in.

When MC1 finally returns home from her quest to kill the evil fae king, nothing will ever be the same again. Because alongside her, holding her newly ringed hand, is the dreaded fae warrior who once stood in her way. The curse has been lifted, the blue skies have returned, crops are growing again, and the human council has nominated her to be permanent envoy to the fae kingdom. In fact, the whole town has come out to see her and her handsome long-eared groom, cheering and throwing streamers. Lastly her father, head of the council, greets them and embraces them both. She must be excited to start her new job? Actually, she politely turns down the offer. She's now developed a love of forest life, and the sprawling estate of her true fae love awaits them. Lastly, the two ride back into the woods, side-by-side, armor gleaming in the sun, and set out to live the life of their dreams. The End.

Turn that into a five or six page scene, and you've got an awww-inspiring happy ever after, and we don't even know all the hardships they faced to get there.

Notice I touched all 5 needs?

Here, I'll do it again.

MC1 is standing in the middle of his little art gallery. Alone. It's opening night. When MC2 walks in, he's carrying drinks, and he hands one to MC1 and tells him to quit looking at his watch. Before long, a few friends come through the door. Some have brought MC1 flowers. MC2 says, 'See? I told you so.' He doesn't leave his side all night, not once. As the hours pass, more and more people arrive, art patrons they've never met before, and now there's a line at the little buffet table. MC1's best friend runs up, and she announces that someone just bought a piece. Their

DJ friend turns up the music. MC1 finally starts to relax and have a good time. Then another piece sells. Then another. Both MCs are over the moon, meeting all sorts of new friends, realizing they now have a serious shot at affording the upstairs flat they're already living in. Finally, MC2 says, 'Come with me.' He drags MC1 into the dark street where it's peaceful and quiet. He turns MC1 toward their place, from where light and cheer spill into the night: a packed gallery. He squeezes him from behind and says, 'You see what you can do?' MC1 sinks into his embrace and finally admits, 'Yes, you did tell me so.' The End.

Two dudes in love, neither rich, just doing their best. And still it has a fairytale feel, doesn't it? Did you spot all 5 needs being met?

Honestly, this is so much fun I'm gonna do another one. Hope that's OK. Here we go.

It's Christmas Eve in small town America. One year after MC1 and MC2 were married. Tonight they're bundled up in the very same gazebo where they said their vows, and the snow has begun to fall. The center of town is dark but for the light outside old Johnson's bakery—and of course the single candle MC2 holds between them. He tells her he can't believe they were ever apart, and he swears by his Purple Heart that he'll never leave her or the town again. She puts a hand on her baby bump and assures him that she knows this is true. She's so glad they have this time alone, but she admits she wishes the kids were there too—hesitantly because they're not his. He kisses her over the candle, and in the middle of it, they hear singing. Soft at first. She looks around and sees half the town coming down the snowy street, everyone carrying candles, singing carols. What a minute, that's the babysitter, who's with the kids? But the kids run out front, dash up the gazebo stairs, and give her a cup of hot chocolate. She turns toward MC2 knowingly. He set the whole thing up. They stand, both taking a hand of each kid, join the town in song, and finish the carol together. The End.

5 needs met, 1 happy ever after accomplished.

Alright, I could do this all day, but you've got books to write. And you have a new technique to practice.

If you want to pull off consistently outstanding happy ever afters, then experiment with creating standalone summaries of your own. Like these. A bunch of them. Using the 5 needs as I did. Brainstorm feel-good scenes that showcase true happiness. Mess around. See what comes up. You'll allude to resolved tensions, but there's no need to get hung up on them, no need to mind the details. Allude to their battles, no more. And just summarize.

Instead of playing that game on your phone or jumping on social media, whip out a few HEA summaries. I promise, if you play with these elements regularly, they will become fun. And once they become fun, you'll be able to write emotionally satisfying, heart-lifting happy ever afters almost every time. Even when it really counts.

Now try it yourself. Use the 5 needs and create your own HEAs. Just. For. Fun.

before we move on: a review

Around the corner we'll bring together the concepts we've covered. By now, I hope you understand the vital roles of romantic tension, likable characters, rising intensity, and even what makes a resounding happy ever after, but one of three questions may still remain:

What the crap do I do with any of it?

Where do I put this stuff, the beginning, the saggy middle, or the big hurrah?

Or more to the point, how does any of this help me write an actual book?

After this page, we'll put things into practice. I have a strong feeling that's why you're here anyways. To build books. Thanks a ton for being patient and reviewing all the building blocks in the previous chapters. They're important. Now it's time to stack them up.

Ready?

part two

Deconstructed Structure Salad

what we talk about when we talk about structure

STRUCTURE IS a romance writer's tool for manipulating romantic tension.

We create romantic fantasies, then we use structure to pace out the fulfillment of those fantasies.

We create romantic goals, then we use structure first to raise hopes and subsequently smash them.

We create a romantic mystery around how happiness could ever be achieved, then we use structure to systematically disconcert, confound, and amaze.

In simplest terms, structure is the way you lay out the parts of your romance. You can look at it from a big picture perspective, like four acts. Or you can zoom in on the specific types of scenes you want in every story, the beats you like to hit, from meet cutes to false highs to long dark nights of the boo-hoo. Either way, you're breaking your story into *parts*.

It's good to think of your story as parts you link together. Each part serves the tension in its own way, and it's your job to make sure those parts line up together.

Some of you follow trusted beat sheets. These come in all shapes and sizes, from reusable ordered lists of scene types to software templates that keep you hitting all the expected scenes and events. They put the parts in prearranged order.

Most good beat sheets have dramatic qualities built into them, the up and down, back and forth. Things are going well for the lovers. Now things are bad. Then they're good again. Now they're worse than ever.

On the other hand, some of you don't use beat sheets at all. And many of you write amazing romances using intuition to feel the roller coaster you're creating. But even though you're not using a preplanned structure, you're still writing wins and then losses, ups and then downs. You're just not using templates to do so. Instead, you've got structure in your gut, and it comes from there. You have a sense of the parts and where they go.

It doesn't matter if you think about structure as a written blueprint or a thing you feel. But it does matter that you think about a story's parts and where to put them.

Let's start by thinking about romance structure on the clearest, most basic level. Once you have that, I will, as usual, complicate the hell out of it.

romance in four sentences

WANT to know the basic structure of romance? I can give it to you in four sentences.

Love is born.
Love gets excited.
Love gets scared.
Love conquers fear.

That's about as simple as you're gonna get, but you know what? It works. Really well. All the beat sheets and templates out there can be refined into those four sentences.

Which equates to four parts.

In a novel, they equate to four acts.

But this also means you can apply the four parts to any length of romance, all the way down to a short story.

Take a look at those four sentences again. Say them aloud, slowly. Don't they just ooze the romance vibe?

No need to wonder why. I'm here. And I explain things.

. . .

Love is born. The first part of any story sets up the status quo—and then wrecks it. Same thing for a romance. We meet our characters, and they meet each other. We see the worlds they live in, what's so great about them, and what's so bad. At least some basics. Then something big happens that rattles their worlds, and things change. Actually two things happen. First, the status quo is upended. Second, the spark of a little somethin' somethin' happens between our characters. They can be friends, enemies, or first-time acquaintances. But an attraction has been established. And curiosities have been set in motion. Also, we see a reason or two why a relationship would never work out. Most importantly, we are 100% sure that nothing will ever be the same.

Love gets excited. Get your glitter pen out and start dotting your i's with hearts. For whatever reason, these two keep bumping into each other. Why? Because they're curious. And curiosity causes people to find reasons to end up in the same room. More and more often. Conversations happen and questions are asked, and the more they hang out, the more they learn about each other, the more curiosity turns into infatuation. Except, the more they learn about each other, the more they realize all the reasons they shouldn't act on their growing heart-throbby feelings. Red flags emerge. Warning signs are everywhere. But guess what? Hot, writhing, aching infatuation wins. Every time. Our lovers turn a blind eye to the warning signs. They can't help it. Impulses are acted upon. Mistakes are made. And nobody is ready for the consequences.

Love gets scared. Oh no. What did they just do? Did they hook up? Did one MC commit to protecting the other no matter what? Did one MC kiss the other on the bridge of her starship in front of all her officers and now the inter-galactic alliance is, like, totally dished? All the reasons our MCs should not do any of that suddenly come crashing back as they come crashing to their senses. Far from a saggy middle, this is where we pour gasoline on all those fires of romantic tension, and our MCs get scared. There's a serious separation, emotionally or physically, and nobody can figure out how to make the relationship work. What's worse, the separation and anxiety make them long for each other even more! Yes, it's best that his rock band left town, but deep down she would do anything to be with him. Happiness felt so close, and now it's gone forever.

Love conquers fear. What, are our characters quitters? Hell no. In this last part, our characters face their fears, their obstacles, all the reasons that kept them apart, and in some major show of love, rise above it all. These are the moments of greatest intensity and hardship. No matter how many types of romantic tension our lovers faced, they resolve them. Usually with profound realizations, metamorphosis, and sacrifice. What are each willing to give up in order to stay together? Here, we *show* the pain and anguish, the trials and consequences, and above all, we show commitment. All the tensions are resolved. All the fears are put to rest. And in the final moments of the story, we allow our lovers peace, a glimpse into the future, the new status quo, and we even get to see that they were right: being together makes it all worth it.

Four sentences. Four parts. Four summaries.

Now, let's get practical. Let's talk specifics. What goes in each of the four parts? Without getting into any exact order of events, below are the things to include.

- **Love is born.**
  - *You introduce your MCs and their everyday lives.*
  - *You plant seeds of several types of romantic tension.*
  - *You start an external plot.*
  - *You make your MCs meet in a memorable way.*
  - *You start the attraction phase.*
  - *You turn their everyday lives upside down.*
  - *You develop a reason your MCs can't get out of the story.*

- **Love gets excited.**
  - *Start the curiosity phase.*
  - *Introduce more types of romantic tension.*
  - *Expose your MCs to each other's power traits.*
  - *Intensify romantic tensions.*
  - *Start the infatuation phase.*
  - *Add more tension intensifiers.*
  - *Bond your MCs with passion and choices.*

- **Love gets scared.**
  - *Intensify romantic tensions.*
  - *Show your MCs struggle and worry.*
  - *Introduce worse romantic tensions.*
  - *Reveal each MC's hidden power trait to each other.*
  - *Create fear and anxiety.*
  - *Separate your MCs significantly.*

- **Love conquers fear.**
  - *Show how bad things have become.*
  - *Present reasons to fight for love.*
  - *Intensify all tensions to a boiling point.*
  - *Create a chance for both MCs to rise above fear.*
  - *Show them making sacrifices and real commitment.*
  - *Wrap up the external plot.*
  - *Show their new status quo and true happiness together.*

. . .

Admittedly, I can't write those without putting them in some kind of order. That almost felt like a beat sheet, didn't it? But within each of the four parts, you *can* play with the sequence. Just keep in mind that entertaining drama staggers the wins and losses. And it orders them with rising intensity. Something good happens. Then something bad. Then something amazing happens. Then something awful.

It really doesn't matter if you put the adhesion moment at the 25% mark. Or the false high at 50%. Or the separation at 75%. Those % markers are easy to follow if you want a re-usable pattern. But you really are free to play. Especially if you understand what those expected scenes do.

And what do they do?

They intensify romantic tension. They are the cans of gasoline we've been talking about this whole time. The biggest ones.

In the next chapter, we'll discuss the common labels of romance scenes and what they do and why we have them. And how they serve the boss, romantic tension.

Some of you, especially non-outliners, might want to stop here. Understanding the four major parts—or acts—of a romance and the way romantic tension fits into them is all you need to write your stories. Awesome. Take some time and get these concepts in your gut. Daydream some stories that follow the four-sentence structure of romance. Then get to writing and being amazing. You already are!

For those who want more details in your prewriting, we'll continue breaking down these parts in the next chapters.

Brace yourself.

the scenes they're looking for

FOR A WHOLE CENTURY, there's been this idea that romances follow a certain pattern of events. There's also been this idea that readers *expect* that certain pattern. Many writers follow it because readers expect it. Many readers expect it because writers follow it. What came first, the chicken or the egg? I don't know. I just like omelettes.

I want to talk about this expected structure a bit. After all, most of the successful beat sheets follow this pattern. What are the expected parts? The expected scenes? And most importantly, why do they work? Then, if you want to use that pattern, you'll know what you're doing. Or if you want to deviate from it, you'll have the confidence and know-how to do so.

Knowledge is power. Grr.

These are the major—and expected—signpost scenes in romance.

- Meet cute
- Adhesion
- False high
- Separation

- <u>Dark moment</u>
- <u>Grand gesture</u>
- <u>HEA</u>

Leave one out, and regular readers of romance will notice. Do them out of order, and the story won't make sense. Maybe the adhesion has some wiggle room, but that's it.

In fact, many romance readers are looking for these scenes. They want to know how you, the creative, will make them interesting and unique. What's *your* take on the meet cute? How dark will *your* dark moment get?

Lucky for everybody, the names of the scenes tell you exactly what happens in them. And it's not difficult to guess in which of the four parts they land. In fact, we've talked about them a whole bunch already; we simply didn't name them as such.

Remember that list of 15 intensifiers of romantic tension? Of that list, these scenes involve the favorite intensifiers of romance connoisseurs. So they get pet names, put into expected scenes, and everyone knows what they're talking about.

Let's break down each of the above signpost scenes. We'll refer back to their corresponding intensifiers. *Because even these expected scenes exist primarily to intensify the romantic tension.* And if you're gonna use these expected scenes, understanding their relationship to the romantic tension will allow you to elevate them beyond expectations.

The <u>meet cute</u> scene corresponds with:

Force it/Adhesion

Emphasize a character with a conflicting goal

Use indirect or confrontational dialogue

Here's the first time your MCs are in the same room. Unless it's second chance or enemies to lovers or such, but you know what I mean. So how do you make it awesome? By adding cute banter and some physical comedy? Sure. But everyone does that. *If you've already decided the types of romantic tension powering your story, then you can start dousing the gasoline right here at the beginning.* If there's **Family/Social Pressure**, make sure at least one of your MCs feels it when they meet. If they're **Actively at Odds**, make sure your readers can sense the potential conflict, even on day one. If there's **Contrary Feelings**, show the inkling of disapproval alongside the attraction. A meet cute intensifies the romantic tension by introducing your MCs, momentarily forcing their proximity, and using heart-pattering dialogue.

The <u>adhesion</u> scene corresponds with:
> *Force it/ Adhesion*
> *Make the status quo less tolerable*
> *Up the stakes*

Let's be totally honest, in a romance you can't have too many reasons to squish your characters together. It's kinda why we're in this game. But this is *the* adhesion moment. This is when they find out that neither can get off the planet. Neither can find another cabin on the ship. Neither can in good conscience let the diabolical land baron close the orphanage and throw all those sweet kids on the street. Or what if one of the MCs *was* that diabolical land baron? Hello external plot, we need a high-stakes reason our potential lovers can't escape this story, thank you. Simply put, your MCs can't get away from each other no matter how many reasons they should. Even if they hate each other. Hehe. Let the fun ensue.

The <u>false high</u> corresponds with:
> *Explore the what if*
> *Make an emotional threat*
> *Up the stakes*

When the infatuation phase peaks, somebody is going to do something big. Maybe something dumb. Maybe something gorgeous. It's like a grand gesture of commitment. Except it's not really for the right reasons, and they're lightyears from resolving the barriers to true love. If there's **Social/Cultural Differences**, their new intimacy will emphasize them. If there's **Internal Resistances**, those are about to be put under a magnifying glass. And if some huge **External Wedge** stands between them, their souls will begin aching terribly. The false high intensifies all that. Stakes increase because they've thrown their lots in together. They lose some of their independence because their paths are now intertwined more than ever. And emotions are threatened because they just got really really vulnerable.

The <u>separation</u> scene corresponds with:
Use indirect or confrontational dialogue
Take something important away
Make an emotional threat
Offer a temptation not to seal the deal
Separation can take many forms. A break-up. A kidnapping. A long angsty silence as their rival bakeries compete for Best Cake in Town. In this scene, all the sources of romantic tension explode together, all the metaphorical cans of gasoline I've been talking about are hucked in at once. Are there resurfacing resentments over **One's Misdeed**? Are the lovers **Actively at Odds** over the same prize? Is the workaholic cop with **Misplaced Feelings** urgently needed to finally solve the case? Verbal fights. Walk outs. Painful choices. Ka-boom, ka-boom, ka-boom. This is the moment your readers feel the most distress for your characters and can't for the life of them figure out how there can ever be a happy ever after. It's that bad. *Again, if you know your sources of romantic tension, then you can be focused and intentional,* and your readers will feel seriously stressed out.

· · ·

The <u>dark moment</u> scene corresponds with:

Use conflicting, unsettling, or provocative imagery
Explore the what if
Up the stakes
Throw in the ticking clock

You want angst? You got it. The separation has happened, and now they're wallowing in it. Distance makes the heart grow absolutely miserable. Not only is the physical separation a metaphor for their relationship, but the uncomfortable settings and imagery can be metaphors for their broken hearts. Why are their hearts broken? Because they're seeing what life is like without each other. Because everything that's wrong in the world will be worse. Because if everything isn't resolved soon, their misery will settle in forever and ever and ever.

The <u>grand gesture</u> corresponds with:

Force it/Adhesion
Emphasize a character with a conflicting goal
Throw in the ticking clock
Pile it on

Oh my gosh, this is the good stuff. Realizations and action. Bravery and commitment. *Sacrifice*. But it doesn't happen in the first paragraph. No, they still need to show up and face obstacles and conquer the external plot—and finally do Big Things for each other. That will take pages. And in those pages, you put them back together, you make the antagonist do his worst deeds, you emphasize that ticking clock yet again, and you make your characters run a shocking gauntlet of fears, obstacles, and treachery. You give them opportunities to prove their love.

The <u>happy ever after</u> corresponds with:

well, none of them

There are no tension intensifiers. Because the tension is gone. Your characters have found peace. And your readers have too. Whether you show life the next day, six months, or two years from now, you want everyone feeling a wonderful sigh of relief. It was worth it. And *needs* are met. And don't rush this. Let your readers spend some time with that peace, hanging with your characters as heart rates return to normal. There is no tension. Not any more

Following a beat sheet will get you these scenes. But knowing that they exist to intensify the romantic tension is a game changer.

Get specific with your types of romantic tension early on. Then these scenes will have purpose. You will have more confidence in how you use them. And your readers will delight in your creative, gasoline-slinging powers.

Soon, I'll walk you through how to plan your own beat sheets. But before that, we have one more structure-related thing to talk about. And we better do it now.

structuring a relationship, or slow-burn vs insta-love

AT SOME POINT, you'll want to know how fast the relationship will go. As in, do they need to cross paths a few times, wait a week before calling, and kiss only on the second date? Or do hot alien pheromones make them immediately explode all over each other in an irrational, uncontrollable, irreversible freak-fest? Or maybe somewhere in between?

You also might ask yourself what your readers expect.

Before long, you'll find yourself comparing slow-burn and insta-love. Put those labels next to each other, and it's easy to tell the difference. And it's easy to pick one.

But once you pick one, you still might be wondering, what exactly does it mean and how do I structure it? If I write slow-burn, do my MCs hook up at 50%, after 75%, or do I make them wait all the way until book two?

Let's take a look at romantic relationships. Break them down in a general sense. And shed some light on the matter.

Below are the four stages of a romantic relationship.

- **Attraction**
- **Curiosity**
- **Infatuation**
- **Love**

Throughout this book I've referred to this list. Did you notice? During the Love is Born, we have attraction. During the Love Gets Excited, we see curiosity emerge, and eventually, infatuation takes over. During Love Gets Scared, things become blocked, and the relationship cannot move forward. But during Love Conquers Fear, the MCs remove those blocks, so love can finally show up and settle in.

A slow-burn romance embraces all the stages. The attraction stage has its own ups and downs. The curiosity stage has its own back and forth. And the infatuation stage, despite its intensity, has ample opportunities to give and take. *Readers of slow-burn enjoy each stage of the relationship*, savoring each nibble along the way like connoisseurs. If you rush from a brief attraction to the peak of the infatuation stage, you'll deny them the nuances.

An insta-love romance, on the other hand, is all about the infatuation stage. Why? Because that's where big mistakes happen, naughty deeds are done, and above all, tensions escalate like a rocket shot through the atmosphere. For many readers, that's the best part. Hence, drawn out attraction and curiosity stages only get in the way—and would be skimmed if they were there. So some romances leave them out almost entirely. In fact, entire sub-genres have been invented to circumvent the first two stages of a relationship, like fated mates and omegaverse.

If you're aiming for the slow-burn crowd, remember to wiggle around within each stage of a romantic relationship, taking your time. Think about how your characters react to each other at each stage. Those readers want to feel the variety.

If you're writing for insta-love fiends, feel free to jump to the infatuation stage in the first part, Love is Born. Throughout most of the story, your MCs will have trouble keeping their hands to themselves and thinking about anything else. If you use more than several types of romantic tension, then you'll have plenty of ways to keep their burning desires frustrated. Just keep a fire extinguisher handy.

Lastly, let's talk about sex. Baby.

I'm going to tell you a very important secret about sex. Ready?

In romance, *sex is not about release*. Instead, sex is a specific kind of *adhesion moment*. Literally. Therefore, sex is—say it with me—*one more tool to intensify romantic tension*.

That's a lot of italics, so you know I'm being serious.

Like any adhesion moment, sex thrusts your MCs together, and the proximity and intimacy exacerbate their issues. And their tissues. .

Clean romance aside, you can include sex early or late or whenever you want. I'd go so far as to argue that sex doesn't dictate whether a romance is slow-burn or insta-love. What dictates those labels is how fast the story moves through the stages of the relationship, not when they hook up. Intimate mistakes can happen at any stage. And those adhesion moments serve to make matters worse not better, to intensify the tension not soothe them.

So remember, in romance sex doesn't fix things. Sex complicates things. Stick it wherever you want, big boy.

This chapter is primarily about the stages of a relationship: its parts. Hopefully, when you lay out the structure of a romance story, you can now put those relationship parts where and when you want them.

bookmark this chapter

AFTER THIS LITTLE REVIEW, we'll get crazy. We'll apply everything so far, and we'll plan a 55K-word romance.

Here's a list of what we've covered. And this is the order we will address them in the following pages.

4 Acts of a Romance Story

- Love is born.
- Love gets excited.
- Love gets scared.
- Love conquers fear.

Stages of a Relationship

- Attraction
- Curiosity
- Infatuation
- Love

. . .

Expected Signpost Scenes

- Meet cute
- Adhesion
- False high
- Separation
- Dark moment
- Grand gesture
- HEA

9 Types of Romantic Tension

- Family/Social Pressure
- Social/Cultural Differences
- Actively at Odds
- One's Misdeed
- Internal Resistance
- Misunderstanding
- Misplaced Feelings
- Contrary Feelings
- External Wedge

Power Traits

- Quick to seize command
- Confident, and therefore unpredictable
- Curious
- Idealistic, passionate, and therefore courageous
- Betrayed, rebellious, and therefore independent

- Altruistic
- Resourceful, clever, and quick thinking
- Experienced and skilled

15 Intensifiers of Romantic Tension

- Use conflicting, unsettling, or provocative imagery
- Take something important away
- Offer a temptation not to seal the deal
- Slip in misdirection or denial
- Explore the what if
- Make the status quo less tolerable
- Emphasize a character with a conflicting goal
- Use indirect or confrontational dialogue
- Force it/Adhesion
- Make an emotional threat
- Up the stakes
- Pile it on
- Sacrifice another character to demonstrate danger
- Make a physical threat
- Throw in the ticking clock

5 Needs for HEAs

- Most basic: food, shelter, rest
- Safety & security: safety from harm, means to get resources, a safe place to call home
- Love & Relationships: friendships, intimacy, family, connections
- Esteem: self-respect, respect from others, community status

- Empowerment: being the best version of one's self, living one's best life

Romance essentials

- Rising intensity
- Up-down, up-down dramatics
- Doors of no return
- A tension-related job for every scene
- Coffee

You now have at your disposal everything you need to brainstorm a powerful, emotionally gripping romance, no matter the genre, the heat level, the genders, or the marketplace.

You can still use a repeatable beat sheet or you can make up your own template.

However, the most empowering skill at your disposal now is the ability to brainstorm romances that are original and authentic every time. *You can now create a custom beat sheet that's tailored to each individual story.*

In the next chapter, we'll practice that skill, step by step, pulling everything together, from romantic tension to structure, and we'll brainstorm a 55K-word novella. We're going to create a beat sheet that's original, packed with all that hair-pulling, nail-biting material, and a total blast to follow as you write. Everything we've been learning up to now has brought you here.

I know you're ready.

Let's do this.

developing your story's unique beat sheet

MANY OF YOU experienced writers might not need this extra hand-holding chapter. But who knows? It might be fun to check out.

First, go back to that early Ice Breaker chapter for a few minutes. Please, just do it. Review those seven bare-bones steps, thinking about all the things we covered since then, types of romantic tension, power traits, intensifiers, and even the stages of a relationship. Do you now have a better understanding of what's going on in each of those seven steps? I could've called it a bare-bones beat sheet, but we weren't there yet. Now we are. It was a simple beat sheet with seven beats.

A 55K-word novella, however, will need more than seven. Yes, but how many? Let's create our unique, customized beat sheet!

Step 1: Calculating your beats

Let's take a novella's average scene length. For lots of us, it's around a pleasant 1800 words. Enough room to work the tension but not enough to bog down the pace of a shorter book. Now do the math. That's about 30 scenes.

Next, there are four acts to a romance. So each act gets roughly seven or eight scenes. Let's say eight because, I don't know, seven just sounds wonky.

We now have a top-down spine for brainstorming and placing everything else. Have a look.

Love is Born
scene 1
scene 2
scene 3
scene 4
scene 5
scene 6
scene 7
scene 8

Love Gets Excited
scene 9
scene 10
scene 11
scene 12
scene 13
scene 14
scene 15
scene 16

Love Gets Scared
scene 17
scene 18
scene 19
scene 20
scene 21
scene 22
Scene 23

scene 24

Love Conquers Fear

scene 25

scene 26

scene 27

scene 28

scene 29

scene 30

scene 31

scene 32

<u>Step 2: The First Twinges: Genre, Characters, & Tropes</u>

For this example, let's pick a fun trope. How about a secret romance? And let's use a setting where secrets are hard to keep, like a small town.

OK, and maybe we want to keep it from getting too dark, so we'll play up the small town vibe and rock the slow-burn. Meaning, we will take our time with both the attraction and curiosity stages and won't introduce the heart-pounding infatuation stage until the middle of Love Gets Excited.

Now we need our characters. How about Daniel and Jackie? Those are sweet small town names. And for some reason, I immediately pictured Daniel behind the wheel of an old busted red pickup truck. So that's gonna happen.

Secret romance has tension built right into it. Therefore, we can start daydreaming why two small town peeps can't tell anyone about it. He works on her farm? Her parents don't like busted red pickup-types? Or maybe she's the newly elected sheriff, the first woman to hold that office, and he's got a criminal past? Whew, those are all good. Let's allow those to percolate a bit while we tinker with those signpost scenes and pacing.

<u>Step 3: Pacing and the Signpost Scenes</u>

In a novella of this length, we don't have a ton of extra scenes, so unlike a full novel, we can justify skipping separate introduction scenes and instead plop the meet cute right at the very beginning. We'll meet both Daniel and Jackie and at the same time offer everyone a few types of romantic tension in scene 1.

We can also add the adhesion early too, the big external plot reason they're stuck in the small town and will very likely keep bumping into each other. *Or* we can delay it until the end of Love is Born. Hmm.

The false high works great at the midpoint; it's so monumental it divides the story in half.

The separation is the climactic bummer that comes at the end of the bummer act, Love Gets Scared. So we'll put it there.

The rest, the dark moment, the grand gesture, and the HEA don't really have many options. Except, let's do the dual POV thing and give both Daniel and Jackie their own dark moments. For the HEA, I want to try a double-header. It's not standard, but let's give our readers a gentle, cozy comedown.

Lastly, in the ten minutes since I wrote it above, that idea of Jackie being the newly elected sheriff and Daniel being recently released from prison totally cemented in my brain. Just think, he's got a bad rep, he's on parole, and guess who he needs to check in with to maintain good standing? Sheriff Jackie. So scene 1 will be their first check in, two days after Daniel's release. Introductions, meet cute, and adhesion, all in one. Bam.

Now our spine will morph into a very basic beat sheet that looks like this:

Love is Born
scene 1 Meet Cute//Adhesion
scene 2
scene 3
scene 4
scene 5
scene 6
scene 7
scene 8

Love Gets Excited
scene 9
scene 10
scene 11
scene 12
scene 13
scene 14

scene 15
scene 16 False High

Love Gets Scared
scene 17
scene 18
scene 19
scene 20
scene 21
scene 22
scene 23
scene 24 Seperation

Love Conquers Fear
scene 25 Dark Moment
scene 26 Dark Moment
scene 27
scene 28
scene 29 Grand Gesture pt 1
scene 30 Grand Gesture pt 2
scene 31 HEA (a week later)
scene 32 HEA (two years later)

<u>Step 4: Brainstorming the Types of Romantic Tension</u>

Well, the prospect of a secret romance has already given us a bunch, even the inklings of some external plot related to law enforcement. Now, let's brainstorm the 9 types of romantic tension and see how many *more* fires we can start for this story. Remember, for a novella, 5 or 6 types is our minimum.

Family/Social Pressure

Jackie is the new sheriff. Daniel is an ex-con. Also, Jackie's dad is a retired sheriff from the town next door. And no doubt she had competition during the election. And geez, a sheriff's office *probably* has rules against getting sweet on parolees under their supervision. Lucky for us, romance readers are really good at suspending disbelief as long as we give them good squee. Basically, everyone in the town will be against this. Too much? Haha, never!

Social/Cultural Differences

Yes, Jackie has a real problem allowing herself feelings for an ex-con. Not only is it a giant professional no-no, but she's spent her life celebrating those on the good side of the law. Also, he's rough around the edges, and she's not used to that. As for Daniel, he's a bit of a drifter and doesn't gel with Jackie's home-town-for-life views.

Actively at Odds

Well, it could get real problematic if Daniel's cellmate had asked him to do some 'favors' once he was out. Is there a little cat-and-mouse between Daniel and Jackie? Man o man, that could crank up the romantic tension. As long as we keep it fun and no innocents get hurt. Let's sit on this possibility for a while.

• • •

One's Misdeed

We need to pick Daniel's original crime. No drugs or murder. But nothing lame either. It needs to be something reprehensible that Jackie will truly have trouble getting over. Maybe he got into a bar fight and put two guys in the hospital? And maybe it was for a bad reason too, like he had a really bad day and simply lost his temper? It's almost relatable, yet not excusable either. For suspense, let's not tell the reader what his crime was for a while.

And what about Jackie? Can we surprise our reader with a time as a deputy she planted evidence on a creep she knew was guilty? Daniel would have a hard time with that—as would the reader.

It's OK, redemption is a thing.

Internal Resistance

Jackie has this inkling feeling that criminals are bad people because, you know, they're criminals. Are they all?

Misunderstanding

No cop and no ex-con will open up 100% to each other right away. Hell no. Their dialogues will be full of half-truths and misleading stories, and that could be a hoot to write. Especially if Daniel has a few 'plans' he's hiding from Sheriff Jackie, and Jackie keeps propping up her perfect sheriff facade. Ouch, lies sting!

Misplaced Feelings

Jackie will be understandably dedicated to her job. For work's sake, she hasn't dated since dumping that other cadet at the academy.

· · ·

Contrary Feelings

The more Daniel gets involved with Jackie, the more he gets frustrated with her insecurities and her unhealthy perfectionism, which has ironically caused some serious imperfections.

And the more Jackie falls for Daniel, the more she discovers that he still has a criminal streak and she could end up resenting him for that.

External Wedge

Maybe Daniel skips town for the week? Violates parole and puts Jackie in an awful bind? Does she pine for him or loathe him? Does she cover up for him or lock him up? Well…all of the above, of course.

Let's plan a physical separation first, then a few scenes later, an emotional one.

First of all, I gotta admit: we have the makings for a rollicking full-length novel. But alas, we've committed to novella.

Second and most importantly, *we absolutely do not need to know the resolution.* We might mistakingly resist a source of tension because it seems too insurmountable. Too difficult. Too unbeliev-able. However, that's a sign our readers will feel the same. *If we can't imagine the HEA at this stage, neither will our readers!* I can't stress this enough: don't be afraid of impossible predicaments.

Let's begin putting these sources of romantic tension along the beat sheet. Not the big conflagrations. Just the sparks of conflict. Just the little introductions of what's to come, little conversations and interactions that let the reader know what's coming. Could we dump them all in scene 1. I guess, but pace them out. Give our readers some time to feel each one's potential for trouble.

Plan scenes that expose and emphasize them. That's the whole purpose of a scene! Remember, the gasoline comes later.

After considering our 9 types for few minutes, how about we leave out Misplaced Feelings and Social/Cultural Differences? Yes, she's dedicated to her work, has to be, but maybe it's not like in an unhealthy workaholic way. And instead of Daniel disliking her hometown-for-life views, instead he loves small town life too; he's just never found a home to settle into.

For simplicity's sake, we'll merely list the types of romantic tension in the beat sheet; it's up to us to remember what we just brainstormed above. Since I'm doing all the talking and these are coming from my imagination, it will be harder for you to memorize; I get it. But give it a whirl.

Also, we'll order them for rising intensity. First scene will be Daniel's POV.

Love is Born
scene 1 Meet Cute//Adhesion//Introduce Tension: Contrary Feelings
scene 2 Introduce Tension: Family/Social Pressure
scene 3 Introduce Tension: Internal Resistance
scene 4
scene 5 Introduce Tension: Actively at Odds
scene 6
scene 7
scene 8

Love Gets Excited
scene 9
scene 10
scene 11 Introduce Tension: One's Misdeed (his)
scene 12
scene 13
scene 14
scene 15

<u>Step 5: Power Traits</u>

Daniel has an anti-authority streak, so *Betrayed, rebellious, and therefore independent.* Lots of criminals have this, but low-lifes also like to play the victim. Not Daniel. He owns his baggage and stands tall, ready make his next move.

And he has no problem taking a risk for the right reason, so *Confident, and therefore unpredictable.*

Eventually, Jackie will see the pattern: the risks he takes are for underdogs and are often for noble reasons, so he's *Idealistic, passionate, and therefore courageous.* This ought to make her reconsider her preconceived ideas about his character. This will be the key to his redemption.

As for Jackie, she's earned her top spot as sheriff, so duh, she's *Quick to seize command.* Daniel has seen plenty of women cops, but not like this.

Also, she's one of the good guys, so she's also *Idealistic, passionate, and therefore courageous.* Wow, a powerful cop with a legitimate heart of gold? However, this will make her misdeed feel more surprising and egregious!

At some point during Love Gets Scared, Daniel will discover and appreciate Jackie's *Curious* side. Always nosing around. Always asking questions. Always finding people to help whom others might not notice.

See? They come from very different worlds, but within fifteen minutes of brainstorming, we imagined traits that, under the right circumstance, line up. Their outer shells conflict. But inside, there's two cores that *need* to be together. Feel it?

Do we know what those right circumstances are yet? Nope. Maybe they'll come to us soon. Maybe we won't know until we write those scenes. That's OK. *If we surprise ourselves, we will likely surprise our readers.*

We can, however, plan scenes that show these traits in action in our beat sheet. And don't forget, up-down, up down for dramatic effect. Since these are up scenes, positive scenes that show attractions and curiosity, let's alternate them between down scenes.

Love is Born
scene 1 Meet Cute//Adhesion//Introduce Tension: Contrary Feelings
scene 2 Introduce Tension: Family/Social Pressure
scene 3 Introduce Tension: Actively at Odds
scene 4 Show Power Trait: Confident, and therefore unpredictable (Daniel)
scene 5 Introduce Tension: Internal Resistance
scene 6 Show Power Trait: Quick to seize command (Jackie)
scene 7
scene 8

Love Gets Excited
scene 9 Show Power Trait: Betrayed, rebellious, and therefore independent
scene 10
scene 11 Introduce Tension: One's Misdeed (Daniel)
scene 12 Show Power Trait: Idealistic, passionate, and therefore courageous (Jackie)
scene 13
scene 14 Reveal Hidden Power Trait: Curious (Jackie)
scene 15
scene 16 False High

Love Gets Scared
scene 17
scene 18 Introduce Tension: One's Misdeed (Jackie)
scene 19 Reveal Hidden Power Trait: Idealistic, passionate, and therefore courageous (Daniel)
scene 20
scene 21 Introduce Tension: External Wedge

scene 22
scene 23
scene 24 Seperation

Love Conquers Fear
scene 25 Dark Moment (Daniel)
scene 26 Dark Moment (Jackie)
scene 27
scene 28
scene 29 Grand Gesture pt 1
scene 30 Grand Gesture pt 2
scene 31 HEA (a week later)
scene 32 HEA (two years later)

Now's a good time to review the breakdown of what goes in each act, found in the chapter Romance in Four Sentences. Compare that to what we have so far.

How are we doing? Do you feel push and pull all over the beat sheet? I sure can.

Step 6: Intensifying the Romantic Tension

Because we know the types of romantic tension, we can be more specific than a generic beat sheet. Do they have doubts? Yes, but exactly what about?

Don't forget that those signpost scenes are intensifiers of romantic tension. That means we have 10 scenes left that need a purpose. That purpose is, of course, to intensify tension. Let's keep exploring that list of 15 Intensifiers. No need to go down the list in order. Let's see what jumps out.

Throw in the ticking clock. What if, instead of recently being elected sheriff, she's up for re-election? That way, any gossip about her will have a more detrimental effect. And there's a set election day right around the corner. The ticking clock will worsen Family/Social Pressure and Jackie's Misdeed.

Make the status quo less tolerable. Daniel will do this. In several stages. He's got a mission to complete, and it's a scooch on the illegal side, so this will affect Jackie's Internal Resistance, their Misunderstandings, and most of all her Contrary Feelings.

Up the stakes. If Jackie actually catches Daniel doing something bad—and she will—she has the power to throw him back in prison. That'll put a big kibosh on their forbidden love. Does he deserve all that, even if they're Actively at Odds? Can she bend the rules for love?

Offer a temptation not to seal the deal. Jackie faces a moment when she can turn her back on Daniel. She can deny their feelings and the relationship and nearly guarantee her re-election. In other words, it's a completely practical time to do the expected thing under the weight of Family/Social Pressure.

Use indirect or confrontational dialogue. Sexy, conflict-filled, subtext-laden banter. Truly, it's going to be in every scene. But let's pick a few times their conversations get especially heated, when they get fired up over Misdeeds, Contrary Feelings, and being Actively at Odds. And don't forget, she has handcuffs.

. . .

That's good for now. Let's place those scenes on our customized beat sheet. Also, since our external plot is still undecided, let's leave a few scenes open near the grand gesture. All of this will give us a top-down beat sheet we can now use to begin writing our novella. Take a look!

Love is Born

scene 1 Meet Cute//Adhesion//Introduce Tension: Contrary Feelings
scene 2 Introduce Tension: Family/Social Pressure
scene 3 Introduce Tension: Actively at Odds
scene 4 Show Power Trait: Confident, and therefore unpredictable (Daniel)
scene 5 Introduce Tension: Internal Resistance
scene 6 Show Power Trait: Quick to seize command (Jackie)
scene 7 Use indirect or confrontational dialogue
scene 8 Throw in the ticking clock

Love Gets Excited

scene 9 Show Power Trait: Betrayed, rebellious, and therefore independent
scene 10 Use indirect or confrontational dialogue
scene 11 Introduce Tension: One's Misdeed (Daniel)
scene 12 Show Power Trait: Idealistic, passionate, and therefore courageous (Jackie)
scene 13 Make the status quo less tolerable
scene 14 Reveal Hidden Power Trait: Curious (Jackie)
scene 15 Use indirect or confrontational dialogue
scene 16 False High

Love Gets Scared

scene 17 Up the stakes
scene 18 Introduce Tension: One's Misdeed (Jackie)

scene 19 Reveal Hidden Power Trait: Idealistic, passionate, and therefore courageous (Daniel)
scene 20 Up the stakes
scene 21 Introduce Tension: External Wedge
scene 22 Use indirect or confrontational dialogue
scene 23 Offer a temptation not to seal the deal
scene 24 Seperation

Love Conquers Fear
scene 25 Dark Moment (Daniel)
scene 26 Dark Moment (Jackie)
scene 27
scene 28
scene 29 Grand Gesture pt 1
scene 30 Grand Gesture pt 2
scene 31 HEA (a week later, after losing election)
scene 32 HEA (two years later, setting up at farmer's market together)

<u>Step 7: The Developmental Edit</u>

Now we sit with our beat sheet. I suggest at least a few days. Me? I write out the scene beats on numbered notecards and begin noting specifics on the back of each. I keep them in my pocket and flip through them often. Or you can leave the beat sheet on your screen and keep scrolling around, going for walks, imagining the scenes, letting the movie in your head develop. Side-plots might emerge too. Side characters and other relationships. Interesting side goals that give Daniel and Jackie more depth. There's plenty of room for those, but they won't ever dominate a scene, not like the romance bits.

This is the best time to do a developmental edit, by the way. You can re-order the scenes now easier than after you've written them. For instance, do the revelations of each character's hidden power trait happen at an appropriate time? Or does the timing of the intensifiers fit the external plot that is finally coming together?

After all, there's still so many ways the story of Daniel and Jackie can go. Whichever direction we chose, this wholly original beat sheet will keep the romantic tension at the forefront, eliminate the saggy middle, and create a hair-pulling, nail-biting mystery about a happy ever after that seems too impossible to happen.

But you know what? It will happen. We just need to figure it out. That's what writers do.

now you do it.

Here are the steps we followed last chapter to create our story's unique beat sheet. It's time you tried it on your own. As always, you might feel clunky the first few times. So don't start with a story you're dying to publish. Make something up from scratch. Remove the pressure. Try to have fun. Eventually, you'll tweak it to fit your process—and make it your own.

- Step 1: Calculating your beats
- Step 2: The First Twinges: Genre, Characters, & Tropes
- Step 3: Pacing and the Signpost Scenes
- Step 4: Brainstorming the Types of Romantic Tension
- Step 5: Power Traits
- Step 6: Intensifying the Romantic Tension
- Step 7: The Developmental Edit

Just like anything else I've asked you to dabble with, the more you try, the more you experiment, and the more you *play*, the more you will learn. In this case, the more you will learn how to create and stoke the fires of romantic tension. You will learn how to create authentic, unique stories that have emotional impact and surprise your readers. And along the way, you'll surprise yourself too.

Maybe you'll develop more confidence in your stories. Maybe you'll feel all those romantic fires in your characters and along their journeys, and they'll re-ignite your own creative spark. Maybe you have all these amazing love stories waiting to get out into the world, unsure just how amazing they are, but now you can help them get there, help them be their best, help them lift the spirits of readers who haven't even heard of you yet.

Continue practicing, not just publishing. Play with your tools. And above all, keep being authentic. Before long, your stories will be as amazing as you.

That's a promise.

thank you

I love sharing what I've learned. Especially about romance. Maybe you could tell how much fun I had writing this book?

It's was almost as fun as sharing it with people directly. Which is truly my passion. You can probably tell that too.

If you want to know more about what I have to share, come find me.

Let's mess around, see what happens!

https://www.coach.me/ChristopherDowning?ref=MogKZ